Bathsheba, An Innocent

Woman?

An Essay Of Refutation On How Bathsheba

Purposely Tempted King David

BY

ANNA D YISRAEL

Published By

Bellevue Publishers

www.BellevuePublishers.com

Special Thanks

I would like to thank my Lord and Savior, Jesus Christ, for inspiring me to write this book, and without which this book wouldn't even exist at all. I would also like to thank my husband, Roeh, for encouraging me every step out of the way of my spiritual journey and throughout my service to the Lord. Finally, I would like to thank my three children, Leah, Maria, and Jethro III, for keeping me down to earth through my God-given motherhood.

ANNA D YISRAEL

INTRODUCTION

M any religions within their own literatures have their fair amounts of heroes, villains, and also a plethora of mythical intrigues that shaped humanity's core beliefs, moral standards, and, for some parts, their own imagination. In Judeo-Christian literature, we must know and understand that the Bible is, in fact, a history book, despite of many miraculous events depicted as providential intervention. Some archeological discoveries are starting to prove that many biblical characters have existed, and even a search in the year 1993 has proven the existence of King David (an ancestor of Christ) and of his own palace. The subject matter of this essay is about one of the king's David wives, Bathsheba, one of the most controversial characters of the Bible. For being seen bathing on her rooftop by King David, who then took her later as his wife in a scandalous adultery, Bathsheba was often depicted as a clever, manipulative, and calculating woman who purposely 'took' her spot next to the king. This essay is coming to her defense and will scripturally prove that Bathsheba, in the great scheme of things, was innocent and never intended to be King David's wife. I will firstly explain and prove that she didn't know that David was going to see her and that David accidentally saw her. I will also explain how she didn't have a choice but to comply with King David's demands, considering the time and era of the event, and how she simply couldn't refuse what he requested of her, even out of goodwill.

Furthermore, I will demonstrate that David was only looking to distract himself and never intended to marry her at first. I will also explain how redemption took place in the midst of their affair and how God forgives David and blesses

Bathsheba by putting her son Solomon on the throne of Israel. Finally, I will compare Bathsheba to the other women of Christ's genealogy and prove that God would have never picked a manipulative woman to be a mother of Christ or, if you prefer, to be a woman in Christ's lineage. That is the part that will pander to your faith a little and make you remember what type of God is the one of the Hebrews, despite of the judgmental, faithless, and worldly standpoint that most of Bathsheba's accusers have against her.

Let's Begin.

AN UNINVITED GUEST

Explains How Bathsheba Didn't Plan

To Be Seen

The Bible starts by describing an intriguing situation: it's the evening, and a woman goes to her rooftop to cleanse herself to complete her purification from her uncleanness. That purification ritual is prescribed by Moses in the biblical book of Leviticus for women who end their menstrual cycle. In this manner, we understand that this woman, who happens to be Bathsheba, is portrayed as an obedient woman to the law by observing this commandment prescribed in the Torah. There is a plot twist, however. At the same time, David, laying down on his bed, has the sudden idea of going out on his rooftop as well. He sees the woman, and she was beautiful to behold. David enquires about the woman and finds out her name and who she's married to.

"And it came to pass in an eventide, that David arose from his bed, and walked upon the roof of the king's house; and from the roof, he saw a woman washing herself; and the woman was very beautiful to look upon. And David sent and enquired after the woman. And one said, Is not this Bathsheba, the daughter of Eliam, the wife of Uriah the Hittite?" (2 Samuel 11:2-3)

Now, according to the cleansing ritual for menstrual cycle purification, there are 8 days to count at each end of a woman's period before she can wash herself from her uncleanness. This alone tells us that she couldn't predict the exact day she was going to be on that rooftop until her period ended. Some scholars accuse Bathsheba of knowing that David would be outside on that evening when the days of her cycle and of her days of purification were unknown to her before her period started. *In other words, if she observed the cleansing ritual prescribed by Moses in the Torah, she couldn't choose the day of that purification, which makes those accusations void of understanding of the somewhat unpredictability of the day she went on her rooftop to wash herself.*

Also, the Scriptures mentioned how David arose from his bed, like something that was not planned as well. If this occurrence had been a habit, I sincerely believe the writer would have specified it. Notice how it says that "it came to pass, at an eventide," letting us know that this choice of his wasn't something scheduled, as some writers have suggested to incriminate Bathsheba's unbelievable timing.

AN UNINTENDED STROLL

Shows how random and unintended David's stroll was

An unusual and unplanned situation strikes again; it's the time for kings to go to war, as the Scriptures say, but David, for an unexplained reason, decides to stay in Jerusalem. We could interpret it as him not supposed to be at home that night.

" (...) at the time when kings go forth to battle, that David sent Joab, and

his servants with him, and all Israel; and they destroyed the children

of Ammon, and besieged Rabbah. But David tarried still at Jerusalem."

(2 Samuel 11:1)

He tarried, it says, which is an interesting choice of words. According to the Oxford Languages dictionary, the word tarry means: "Stay longer than intended; delay leaving a place". David staying longer than he was supposed to made him unexpectedly see Bathsheba bathing and, thus, was tempted at her sight. Could we just humble ourselves and admit that this situation is greater than Bathsheba and David themselves? Could it be that the stars were aligned for such an occurrence, and nothing could be done to stop it? We do know, however, that God doesn't tempt anyone (James 1:13). So, what happened? Only God knows...

But anyway, we can also suggest that Bathsheba assumed, knowing the time of the year (kings going to war, according to 2 Samuel 11:1), that David was absent from his house, which made her take such a risky chance. We know she kept the law of Moses, through observing the Levitical prescriptions, so it's farfetched to say that such a God-fearing woman would calculate such a plot.

Henceforth, David wasn't supposed to be there, which would be common sense to conclude that his life-changing stroll wasn't planned and that Bathsheba couldn't obviously know he would be there as well. But let's continue.

A CALL FOR LUST

Argues how David only wanted to "borrow" Bathsheba for a night, and never intended to "steal" her form her husband Uriah

" And David sent messengers and took her, and she came in unto him, and he lay with her; for she was purified from her uncleanness: and she returned unto her house" (2 Samuel 11:4)

Clearly, David was burning for lust for that married woman and sent messengers to have her for a night. He was just going to have her for pleasure and not trying to have a child with her. However, as the God-fearing woman Bathsheba was, things didn't go as planned for David (again!), and Bathsheba got pregnant. If David was trying *to steal Bathsheba from Uriah, he would have eliminated him as soon as he learned she was pregnant, but no. Instead, David tries to cover up the whole thing by trying to send Bathsheba's husband back to his house so her husband could lie with her and have this pregnancy pass as Uriah's seed.*

"And David said to Uriah, Go down to thy house, and wash thy feet. And Uriah departed out of the king's house (...)"
(2 Samuel 1:8)

This sticky situation is the evidence that David only had the desire to have Bathsheba for a night. But since things didn't go as planned for David, and Bathsheba got pregnant, King David had to find a way to camouflage his adultery and make Bathsheba's unborn child pass as Uriah's. Now, we know that David never intended to kill Uriah to take his wife at first. But again, the situation gets messier: things derailed again. Uriah, for some mysterious latent reason, never went back to his house despite several occasions that David gave him to do so.

Bathsheba, An Innocent Woman?

"But Uriah slept at the door of the King's house with all the servants of his lord and went not down to his house. And when they had told David, saying, Uriah went not down unto his house, David said to Uriah, Camest thou not from thy journey? Why then didst thou not go down unto thine house?" (2 Samuel 11:9)

"And David said to Uriah, Tarry here today also, and tomorrow, I will let thee depart. (...)

(2 Samuel 11:12)

"(...) and at the even, he (Uriah) went out to lie on his bed with the servants of his lord, but went not down to his house." (2 Samuel 11:13)

Here, we see that King David gave several occasions to send Uriah to his house. But for some incomprehensible reasons, Uriah always tarries and fails to go back to his house despite of a kingly order. At this point, we can say that an invisible and mysterious force is preventing Uriah from obeying the king, and now, both the lives of King David and Bathsheba *are in danger. This adultery act can be discovered, which is, in ancient Israel, a transgression punishable by death.*

"And the man that committeth adultery with another man's wife, even he that commiteth adultery with his neighbour's wife, the adulterer and the adulteress shall surely put to death."

(Leviticus 20:10)

At this point, Bathsheba's pregnancy is on the brink of being discovered, as well as David's adulterous act, so the situation takes a new turn. To save his life from the deadly punishment of the law, David is forced to go on his next move, which is to have Uriah killed to cover up his adultery.

FATAL COVER UP

Demonstrates how David chose to kill Uriah to cover up his scandalous act

As mentioned before, the punishment by law in ancient Israel for sleeping with another man's wife is death. David tried to camouflage Bathsheba's adulterous pregnancy by sending her husband, Uriah, back home on several occasions, but with no success. It is now to the point where David's affair with Bathsheba is at the margin of being discovered, so David attempts to save his life by setting up Uriah to have him killed.

"And it came to pass in the morning that David wrote a letter to Joab, and sent it by hand of Uriah. And he wrote in the letter, saying, Set ye Uriah in the forefront of the hottest battle, and retire from him, that he may smitten, and die." (2 Samuel 11: 14-15)

Here, we understand that David tried many times to cover up his adultery and wash his hands from his unlawful act with Bathsheba. Alas, for him, that didn't work out for him so he finally decides to get rid of Uriah. An unpopular observation to this whole situation is to acknowledge that an order of a king should always be followed and that if Uriah only obeyed the king, his life would have been spared. However, it seems that God had other plans for Bathsheba, a fearful woman.

The reason why Bathsheba is considered fearful is because she didn't resist David's advances, knowing that nothing is to be refused to the king, in those times at least. Many scholars misunderstood the time era in which Bathsheba and David lived and failed to realize that any disobedience to the king could be sentenced by death. The kingdom of ancient Israel wasn't a democracy. We must look at David's advances as an order from the government and not as something that could've been easily dismissed. But modern scholars seem to perceive David's kingdom as a modern-day democracy, which is a terrible mistake. After all, didn't Uriah lose his life for disobeying the king in some manner? But let's continue.

THE FIFTEEN MINUTES WIDOW

A pregnant Bathsheba, after she loses her husband, gets married to King David

This time, David's mischievous plan works; Uriah goes to war in the forefront of the hottest battle and loses his life. Nevertheless, when Bathsheba learns the news of her dead husband, she doesn't rejoice, as a calculating Bathsheba would. She mourned according to the Scriptures. The Bible says that the mourning period for someone in grief shouldn't exceed seven days. After Bathsheba's mourning, David took her as his wife.

We could assume here that he took her since she bore him a child and that it was the indicated gesture to do in this situation. A child of an anointed king should never be put away, so David, once again, had to take her, which wasn't his original plan as we know now. But Bathsheba was a God-fearing woman who observed the Torah, so God didn't abandon her in the midst of her trial. The Scriptures doesn't specify how long she had been married to Uriah before she married David, but also it doesn't mention that she had children from Uriah as well. We could interpret it as if Bathsheba didn't have any children from Uriah yet, and that the child from David's seed was her firstborn. But that's just a plausible hypothesis.

Now that Bathsheba is newlywed to King David, she is now in the king's house, but her troubles wouldn't end there. A judgment from the Highest will be declared against David for Uriah's murder. Bathsheba will experience trouble as well since her life is now intertwined with David's from that day on.

Would a calculating woman risk her whole life for the sake of just being the king's wife? Also, knowing the fact that

David had other wives before her and sons from them who were better ranked in the line of succession, we simply cannot believe that Bathsheba was that foresighted. Nothing at this point could directly and with no shadow of a doubt assure that her future children could rise so high in succession. She didn't know if her children would be physically or mentally impaired or simply unfit to rule. If some scholars really think she was that mathematically good at calculating such an outcome, then they should also stop seeing her as an unimportant biblical character because such an ability to predict the future deserves a higher level of respect for a biblical character who is often thrown under the bus. But let's see what Bathsheba and David had to go through for being married to each other after an adulterous act.

PAYING FOR IT

Shows how God punishes the newlywed

couple for committing adultery

S ome unbelievers would think that King David got rid of Uriah, married his wife, and had many children with her in the end. But not so! The Lord sends the prophet Nathan to let David know that his whole plot was known and unpleasant unto Him, and that He was about to punish David for his crime. The prophet, however, uses an analogy of a man who had many flocks and who took another man's lamb, which was his only one. King David, not knowing that the analogy was referencing to him and Uriah, gets greatly angry at this man and orders this to Nathan:

"As the Lord liveth, the man shall surely die; And he shall restore the lamb fourfold, because he did this thing, and because he had no pity" (2 Samuel 12:5-6)

But Nathan tells David that he is the man from the analogy. For this matter, Nathan announces a curse from the Lord on David's house. The sword would always be set against his whole house. After, David loses the newborn child he conceived with Bathsheba, and furthermore, one of his sons will lie with David's concubines later in history.

A REDEMPTION STORY

Demonstrates how God forgives David,

as well as using Bathsheba to birth the

future king of Israel

After the loss of their first child, David and Bathsheba come together again and conceive a second one. This time, the child lives and is called Solomon. God forgives David's trespasses, decides to recognize the child, and graces him with His love.

"And David comforted Bathsheba, his wife, and went in unto her, and lay with her; and she bare a son, and he called his name Solomon: and the Lord loved him." (2 Samuel 12:24)

Solomon grew and was eventually chosen by the Lord Himself to be the future ruler of Israel after his father, David. But this wouldn't take place easily. Solomon would have to face a rival, his own brother Adonijah and once more, the life of Bathsheba is put at stake. An acute reader would understand at this point that Bathsheba couldn't willfully put her life in danger again. Also, she couldn't possibly predict how victorious she would be. Her obedience to prominent men as King David and Prophet Nathan confirmed her submissive nature to the order of things, which once again protected her life. In the story, the anointed prophet Nathan tells Bathsheba what to do to save herself.

"Wherefore, Nathan spake unto Bathsheba the mother of Solomon, saying, Hast thou not heard that Adonijah the son of Haggith doth reign, and David our lord knoweth it not? Now therefore come, let me, I pray thee, give thee counsel, that thou mayest save thine own life, and of thy son Solomon"(1 Kings 11-12)

Is Bathsheba calculating? No. Is she obedient, however? Yes, which is why the Most high could use her on such a higher level. Henceforth, notice how that part we just read wasn't from her alone but was the idea from an anointed man of God, the beloved prophet Nathan. I sincerely believe that the people who accused Bathsheba of being manipulative totally dismissed how highly cooperative she was, which is why she has been led so far in her journey.

SOLOMON THE KING

Shows how God gives Bathsheba the honor and victory of having her son on the throne

It's no secret that Solomon, Bathsheba's son, will finally be chosen by his father, David, to be crowned king of Israel. We can assume that God, by noticing Bathsheba's incredible submission and obedience to anointed men of the Most High, elected Bathsheba to be the mother of David's successor to the throne. The *Gebirah*, which is a Hebrew term to describe the mother of the king or the "queen mother," is a title that held very high importance and honor in the times of the Israelite kings, especially in the Davidic dynasties.

Knowing how cooperative and submissive Bathsheba was, God granted her a place in the king's court, which is a very exceptional place for a woman in such a patriarchal system like in those days. Some could foresee Bathsheba as a feminist figure, one of a woman who was given a voice in a male-dominated world. She could directly speak to the king, and she had a place next to him by his throne. The Gebirah could have her requests submitted and accepted by the king.

"Bathsheba therefore went unto king Solomon, to speak unto him for Adonija. And the king rose up to meet her, and bowed himself unto her, and sat down on his throne, and caused a seat to be set for the king's mother; and she sat on his right hand." (1 Kings 2:19)

What an honorable position that was given to Bathsheba, that was the wife and the mother of righteous men, despite of their known shortcomings. Moreover, she was at the right *hand of the king, which is a position usually reserved for royal counselors and/or advisers. We must remember that Solomon was loved of the Most High and that by elevating a man He loved, He also elevated that man's mother. Here, some could see a prefiguration of Christ and his mother, Mary, in the Kingdom of Heaven.*

A MOTHER OF CHRIST

Finally, how Bathsheba is triumphantly one of the only five female ancestors of Christ mentioned in the New Testament

Victory! Despite of all her trials and tribulations, Bathsheba is not only chosen by God to be one of Christ's ancestors but she is also given the honor of being one of the five women mentioned in Christ's genealogy in the New Testament.

"And Jesse begat David the king; and David the king begat Solomon of her that had been the wife of Urias (...)" (Matthew 1:6)

Now, her name is not explicitly mentioned, but she is one of the only five women mentioned in Christ's genealogy, along with Thamar, Rachab, Ruth, and Mary. We can understand through this insertion how meaningful and powerful Bathsheba is. If we study the other women mentioned, we notice how strong, virtuous, and dignified they are. Ultimately, these women showed a great level of obedience to whoever covered them, and that's why we could assume why Bathsheba received the honor of being pointed out.

As a matter of fact, we cannot imagine that a manipulative and calculating woman would have been given this much honor in the Israelite community. That's a matter of knowing how the ancient Israelites perceived women and what made them select them to be glorified. Being a female in Christ's genealogy is being his ancestor, and being his ancestor is being his mother. We can declare that Bathsheba is a mother of Christ since her blood is flowing in his veins (remember, Christ is still alive!) and that Bathsheba is a part of Christ himself.

Denying this is denying the faith, which would make us worse than infidels. If Christ would have to come tomorrow, Bathsheba would be alive standing around him as a resurrected and redeemed ancestor of his and as a very honorable queen mother descending through his bloodline.

CONCLUSION

B athsheba is, *without a shadow of a doubt, one of the most controversial biblical characters. Many have perceived her as a seductive, manipulative woman, when others saw her as an insignificant, naïve figure. This essay was to establish that she was neither. By searching the Scriptures thoroughly, I came to find that Bathsheba was, in fact, a God-fearing woman who was simply obedient, submissive, and cooperative in any given situation. Many tend to forget how she suffered through her journey by losing a husband a son, and losing another husband, David, when Solomon became king. It is a little bit disconnected from reality to believe that she had planned her promotion when nothing was in her control. The day of her purifying*

bath was determined by the Levitical law by counting eight days to wash herself after her issue had stopped. Then, when David went to get her, she couldn't do otherwise but to comply, given the fact that it was an order from the king. Technically, his desires are orders. Finally, when her son Solomon almost lost the throne, she followed every instruction that came from the prophet Nathan, another fearful man of the Most High. She just showed how submissive she was. A lot of people underestimate the power of a submissive woman in a patriarchal world. Perhaps that submission in a woman is the only way that leads to a woman's liberation, by following through orders all the way to become a voice among men. Bathsheba is the perfect example of how obedience can make you promoted, as she became the queen mother (Gebirah) in the time of her son Solomon. Let's meditate, for that matter, on how submission can lead women to liberation and to so much more, redemption.

BIOGRAPHY

Born in 1982, Anna D Yisrael is a woman who was always passionated about the Holy Bible. With a Catholic background and upbringing,she later joined the Hebrew Israelite Community in 2014. She now has a podcast where she teaches topics that are essentially centralized on women and biblical themes pertaining to them. She has a Vocational College Degree in Psychology and Social Studies, a Technical College Degree in Preschool and Elementary Education and she also studied History of Art and Communication at the University.

www.ingramcontent.com/pod-product-compliance
Lightning Source LLC
Chambersburg PA
CBHW051251120626
46547CB00014B/1890